Poetry in Motion

Poetry in Motion

Galerie BEYELER
June 12th-September 15th, 2007

Gallery HYUNDAI
October 2nd-October 14th, 2007

Georg Baselitz

Alexander Calder

Sam Francis

Rebecca Horn

Robert Indiana

Roy Lichtenstein

Sigmar Polke

Robert Rauschenberg

Gerhard Richter

Frank Stella

Sang-Hwa Chung

Tschang-Yeul Kim

Whan-Ki Kim

Ufan Lee

Sang-Kyoon Noh

John Pai

Nam-June Paik

Seo-Bo Park

Sung-Hy Shin

Se-Ok Suh

Poetry in Motion

by Garett E. Marshall

A close association between art and poetry has long existed in both Western and Eastern civilizations. This seemingly universal association comes naturally, for both art and poetry are essentially individual expressions and manifestations of emotions and thoughts emerging from life's circumstances and experiences. Both strive to convey man's relationship with himself, with others and with the world around him, and both require an imaginative sensitivity in pursuing a distinctive style and rhythm.

Throughout much of history in all cultures, artists and poets were largely restricted by the formal rigidities of convention and didacticism. However, in modern times they have increasingly been released from such strict controls on subject matter, composition, style and rhythm. While artists today predominantly continue to pursue their work with paint and brush on canvas and poets through verse with pen on paper, they have devised and borrowed varying methods and materials ultimately to achieve a shared objective - to explore and expand upon their feelings and ideas and to share their contemporary experiences with others. No longer caged in, they are, thus, able to unleash their creative force in any direction and to employ every means to their satisfaction.

This unleashing does not mean that all artists and poets have abandoned their culture and traditions, but that they are not restrained by their heritage. In fact, some artists and poets have purposely dedicated themselves to rediscovering, preserving, reinterpreting and even reworking their own cultures and traditions and taking them in new directions. At the same time, other artists and poets have gone on to explore new realms of creativity and expression and have even gained inspiration from cultures and traditions different from their own: subject matters, materials and techniques once considered taboo or simply unknown are now the sustenance of artists and poets alike the world over. As a result, both intensity and universality are distinctively achieved in art and poetry: figuratively, metaphorically, abstractly, conceptually, minimally, rhythmically or arrhythmically.

Always tied to this intensity are the discipline and the dedication artists and poets give to their life journeys - very personal experiences that they feel compelled to share through their creative expressions and statements. No matter how distinctive or singular their art or poetry may be or how steeped in their own world it is, a universal connection is certainly attainable. Because the viewer or reader brings to the work his own life experiences, emotions and thoughts, limitless opportunities exist in which to connect, interpret and find meaning. In this way, just as a picture, painting or sculpture can be worth a thousand words, so can a poem be worth a thousand images.

What makes a painting or sculpture art? What makes a poem poetry? Given that contemporary art and poetry have largely been freed from fixed notions, structures and purposes, far greater room is now available for discussion and disagreement about what makes art great or poetry great and even what is and what is not art or poetry. The test of time, of course, and how succeeding generations choose to embrace, reject or simply pass over what is handed down to them are always part of the equation in determining the masterwork. But also existing is the test of cross cultural understanding and appeal. Moreover, technology has certainly expedited and advanced the possibilities for this determination of quality in our time.

Still, we pass down from generation to generation and we give and take from culture to culture the accumulation of all that constitutes who we are individually and collectively. This process is not always smooth or easy, nor is it always for the better. Much is gained and perhaps much is lost in the handing down and the sharing. Nevertheless, every generation and each culture will add to and take away from this accumulation according to their own needs and desires. Ultimately, though, our art and poetry and other creative accomplishments are the most precious heirlooms that we have to share, preserve and bequeath. As John Keats, the English poet, reminds us about the permanence of artistic expression: "Beauty is truth, truth beauty - that is all ye know on earth, and all ye need to know."

With these thoughts in mind, this collection of works by artists from different places and generations and from varying circumstances and perspectives has been assembled under the title Poetry in Motion. The purpose is to offer the viewer an opportunity to take pause and simply encounter in his own way and from his own experience and worldview the visually poetic and eclectic expressions of these artists. One part of the collection is made up of ten world-renowned artists whose works have been frequently exhibited at Galerie Beyeler and will be familiar to most visitors. The other part of the collection is made up of ten Korean artists whose works selected by Gallery HYUNDAI are being shown for the first time at Galerie Beyeler and will most likely be a new encounter for most visitors. A selection of poems has been added to this catalogue to further enhance and complement the works and concept of this exhibition.

To live the life of an artist or poet may seem a remote thought to many of us. Perhaps it has always been this way. Still, within all of us is the ability to live an artistic and poetic life and to allow creativity to be woven into our life patterns. Such an experience in life is as simple as viewing a work of art or reading a poem and allowing that experience to enhance our own life journey whether intellectually or emotionally. Sometimes, we instantaneously comprehend and connect with an artist or poet's intent. Sometimes, this understanding happens gradually; sometimes it never does. However, whether revisiting works by artists we have long known or being introduced to works by artists we have never seen, we are more likely than not to gain something pertinent, meaningful and beautiful by simply taking the time and effort to step back, take pause and approach the experience openly.

In this hectic world, we are immersed in demanding, everyday responsibilities and "the world," as the poet William Wordsworth suggests, "is too much with us." But in such things as art and poetry we can still seek refuge, find solace and nourish our minds and spirits. Correspondingly, the inspiration for this exhibition is to offer the viewers art that may be familiar along side art that may not be so familiar in order to provide the opportunity to approach both of them with the simple idea of art being poetry in motion as a celebration of free verse and artistic expression.

In modern times, a full range of feelings and thoughts can be openly experienced and shared across culture and time whether they are concrete or abstract, presented in meter or verse, achieved through rhyme or meditative discipline, or through onomatopoeias and the unrestricted strokes of a brush. Key to the aesthetics of language in poetry and form in art is the presence of motion - whether this motion is fast paced and energetic or so slow that it is almost indiscernible. By visually reading works of art like poetry, we can gain insight into the thoughts and emotions of the artists and appreciate the rhythms they achieve through the use of their hands - whether these motions are steady, precise and repetitive or free flowing, unfettered and unique. The collection of art presented here by both Western and Korean artists offers a bit of both.

The poetic motion found in the works by the Korean artists largely embodies a meditative repetition that comes from a spiritual journey and is rooted in East Asian philosophy and aesthetics evident in traditional Eastern brush painting. While the individuality of each artist's pursuit is apparent in the diversity of their work, a contemplative purity and poetic sentiment can be found in their Korean identity that binds them together. Such contemporary lyricism, often imbued with nostalgia, beats rhythmically through their varied use of both Eastern and Western techniques and materials. Many of these Korean-born artists have, in fact, spent substantial periods of their lives studying, working and living in Western countries, yet all have maintained close ties to their motherland. Consequently, the extensive exposure to Western art concepts and styles they have had has served to strengthen, not dilute, their Korean identity.

The artistic accomplishments of all the artists included in this exhibition - regardless of their country of origin - connect us to their individual life journeys, exquisitely replicate the rhythms and harmony of the space and time they have occupied and echo the cultural heritages from which they come, inviting us to move with them.

Poetry in Motion

Garett E. Marshall

Seit langem besteht – in westlichen wie in östlichen Kulturen – eine enge Beziehung zwischen Kunst und Dichtung. Dieser scheinbar universelle Zusammenhang ist ganz natürlich, schließlich sind Kunst und Dichtung im wesentlichen Äußerungen von Emotionen und Gedanken, die sich aus den Umständen und Erfahrungen des Lebens ergeben. In beiden Bereichen geht es darum, dem Verhältnis des Menschen zu sich selbst, zu anderen und zu seiner Umwelt Ausdruck zu verleihen, und hier wie da bedarf es phantasievollen Feingefühls, um einen bestimmten Stil und Rhythmus zu entwickeln.

In der Geschichte sämtlicher Kulturen kam es immer wieder vor, dass Künstler und Dichter durch die starren Formalitäten der Konvention und übertriebener Didaktik erheblich eingeschränkt waren. In neuerer Zeit jedoch haben sie sich zunehmend von diesen rigiden Kontrollen über Thematik, Komposition, Stil und Rhythmus befreit. Auch heute noch arbeiten Künstler zwar überwiegend mit Farbe und Pinsel auf Leinwand, so wie Dichter ihre Verse mit dem Stift zu Papier bringen, doch haben sie unterschiedliche Methoden und Materialien entwickelt oder übernommen, um letztlich ein gemeinsames Ziel zu erreichen – sie wollen ihre Gefühle und Ideen erforschen und kundtun, wollen ihre Erfahrungen als Zeitgenossen mit anderen teilen. Befreit von derlei Zwängen, sind sie heute in der Lage, ihre kreativen Kräfte in jeder Richtung zu entfalten und dazu jedes Mittel beliebig einzusetzen.

Diese freie Entfaltung bedeutet allerdings nicht, dass alle Künstler und Dichter ihre Kultur und ihre Traditionen aufgegeben hätten, sondern vielmehr, dass deren Erbe sie nicht mehr behindert. Tatsächlich haben sich ja manche Künstler und Dichter ganz bewusst daran gemacht, ihre eigenen Kulturen und Traditionen wiederzuentdecken, zu bewahren, neu zu interpretieren und sogar umzuarbeiten und ihnen eine neue Richtung zu geben. Zugleich haben andere Künstler und Dichter begonnen, neue Sphären der Kreativität und des Ausdrucks zu erforschen, und sich sogar von Kulturen und Traditionen inspirieren zu lassen, die nicht die ihren sind: Stoffe, Materialien und Techniken, die früher tabuisiert wurden oder einfach unbekannt waren, bilden heute die Quelle für Künstler und Dichter auf der ganzen Welt. So kommt es, dass in der Kunst wie in der Dichtung Intensität und Universalität auf spezifische Weise erzielt werden: figurativ, metaphorisch, abstrakt, konzeptuell, minimal, rhythmisch oder arhythmisch.

Diese Intensität geht stets einher mit der Disziplin und dem Engagement von Künstlern und Dichtern bei der Beschreibung ihres individuellen Lebenswegs – sehr persönliche Erfahrungen, die durch ihre kreativen Äußerungen und Statements mitzuteilen ihnen ein Bedürfnis ist. Unabhängig vom spezifischen Charakter ihrer Kunst oder Dichtung und unabhängig davon, wie stark sie von ihrer eigenen Welt durchdrungen sein mögen – eine universelle Verbindung ist sicherlich im Rahmen des Möglichen. Angesichts der Tatsache, dass der Betrachter oder Leser ja seine eigenen Lebenserfahrungen, Emotionen und Gedanken in das Werk einfließen lässt, sind die Chancen, Bedeutung zu assoziieren, zu interpretieren und zu finden, praktisch grenzenlos. In diesem Sinne kann nicht nur ein Bild – Gemälde oder Skulptur – so viel wert sein wie tausend Wörter, sondern auch ein Gedicht so viel wie tausend Bilder.

Wodurch wird ein Gemälde oder eine Skulptur zu Kunst? Wodurch wird ein Gedicht zu Lyrik? Da die zeitgenössische Kunst und Dichtung sich weitgehend von starren Begriffen, Strukturen und Zwecken befreit haben, lässt sich heute in einem sehr viel breiteren Rahmen über die kontroverse Frage diskutieren, was Kunst oder Dichtung groß macht, ja, was Kunst oder Dichtung eigentlich sind, beziehungsweise nicht sind. Ausschlaggebend für die Definition eines Meisterwerks ist natürlich stets das zeitliche Kriterium, also die Art und Weise, wie nachfolgende Generationen sich das, was ihnen überliefert wurde, zu eigen machen, verwerfen oder schlicht und einfach übergehen. Doch genauso gibt es das Kriterium eines wechselseitigen Verständnisses, einer wechselseitigen Anziehungskraft zwischen den Kulturen. Zudem hat die Technik unserer Zeit fraglos dazu beigetragen, die Möglichkeiten dieser Art von Qualitätsbestimmung zu fördern und voranzutreiben.

Und dennoch ist doch alles, was unser individuelles und kollektives Sein ausmacht, eine Akkumulation von Werten, die wir von Generation zu Generation weitergeben, von Kultur zu Kultur übernehmen. Dieser Prozess des Gebens, Nehmens und Teilens verläuft nicht immer glatt und reibungslos, auch führt er nicht immer zwangsläufig zu einer Verbesserung. Viel wird dabei gewonnen, aber vieles kommt vielleicht auch abhanden. Gleichwohl wird jede Generation und jede Kultur – entsprechend ihren Bedürfnissen und Wünschen – diesen Fundus ergänzen und sich aus ihm bedienen. Letztlich allerdings sind unsere Kunst und Dichtung oder andere kreative Leistungen die kostbarsten Erbstücke, die wir miteinander zu teilen, zu bewahren und zu überliefern haben. Erinnern wir uns an die Worte des englischen Dichters John Keats, der über die Permanenz des künstlerischen Ausdrucks sagt: „Schönheit ist Wahrheit, Wahrheit Schönheit – das ist alles, was ihr wisst auf Erden und alles, was ihr wissen müsst."

Mit diesen Reflexionen wurde die Sammlung dieser Werke, die aus unterschiedlichen Orten und Generationen stammen, in unterschiedlichen Situationen und Perspektiven entstanden sind, unter dem Titel „Poetry in Motion" zusammengestellt. Ziel ist es, dem Betrachter so etwas wie eine Atempause zu verschaffen: Er soll die Möglichkeit erhalten, sich auf seine Weise, aus seiner persönlichen Erfahrung und Weltsicht mit den visuell poetischen und eklektischen Äußerungen dieser Künstler zu konfrontieren. Der eine Teil der Sammlung besteht aus Werken von zehn Künstlern, die wiederholt in der Galerie Beyeler ausgestellt wurden und den meisten Besuchern vertraut sein dürften. Der andere Teil der Sammlung vereinigt die Arbeiten zehn koreanischer Künstler, die erstmals in der Galerie Beyeler gezeigt werden und für die meisten Besucher eine Neuentdeckung sein dürften. Eine zusätzliche Auswahl von Gedichten im Katalog soll dazu dienen, die von der Gallery HYUNDAI ausgewählt werden, und die Werke und das Konzept dieser Ausstellung zu bereichern und zu ergänzen.

Das Leben eines Künstlers oder Dichters zu führen mag vielen von uns als etwas Abwegiges erscheinen. Vielleicht war das immer schon so. Und dennoch, in jedem von uns ist die Fähigkeit zu einem Künstler- und Dichterdasein angelegt, jeder von uns kann Kreativität in seine Lebensmuster einfließen lassen. Eine solche Erfahrung im Leben zu machen ist genauso einfach wie ein Bild zu betrachten oder ein Gedicht zu lesen und den eigenen Lebensweg intellektuell oder emotional um diese Erfahrung zu bereichern. Manchmal begreifen wir die Absicht eines Künstlers oder Dichters auf Anhieb und sind in der Lage, uns mit ihr zu identifizieren. Manchmal vollzieht sich dieses Verständnis nur schrittweise; manchmal auch gar nicht. Doch egal, ob wir Werke eines Künstlers, die wir seit langem kennen, neu betrachten oder ob wir Werken von Künstlern, die wir nie gesehen haben, zum ersten Mal begegnen – es ist mehr als wahrscheinlich, dass uns etwas Angemessenes, Bedeutsames und Schönes zuteil wird, wenn wir uns einfach die Zeit nehmen und die Mühe machen zurückzutreten, einzuhalten und uns unvoreingenommen auf die Erfahrung einlassen.

In dieser hektischen Welt sind wir tagtäglich schwierigen Verantwortungen ausgesetzt, „die Welt ist", wie der Dichter Willam Wordsworth schreibt, „zu sehr mit uns". Doch in Sphären wie der Kunst und Dichtung können wir nach wie vor Zuflucht suchen und Trost finden, Nahrung für unseren Geist und unsere Seele. In diesem Sinne versteht sich denn auch unsere Ausstellung: Sie will die Betrachter mit vertrauter und nicht so vertrauter Kunst konfrontieren und ihnen damit die Möglichkeit bieten, sich der einen wie der anderen mit der einfachen Vorstellung zu nähern, dass Kunst nichts anderes ist als Dichtung in Bewegung. Was hier zelebriert wird, sind freier Vers und künstlerischer Ausdruck.

Heutzutage lassen sich unterschiedlichste Gefühle und Gedanken über kulturelle und zeitliche Schranken hinweg offen erfahren und mitteilen, egal ob sie konkret oder abstrakt sind, ob sie sich in Metren oder Versen präsentieren, durch Rhythmus oder meditative Disziplin erzielt werden oder durch Lautmalereien und die freie Entfaltung von Pinselstrichen. Entscheidend für die Ästhetik der Sprache in der Dichtung und der Form in der Kunst ist die Präsenz von Bewegung – wobei es keine Rolle spielt, ob diese Bewegung schnell und energisch ist oder so langsam, dass sie sich kaum wahrnehmen lässt. Indem wir Kunstwerke visuell lesen wie Dichtung, können wir Einblicke in die Gedanken und Emotionen der Künstler gewinnen und die Rhythmen erfassen, die unter dem Einsatz ihrer Hände zustande kommen – wie immer diese Bewegungen auch geartet sein mögen: stetig, präzise und repetitiv oder frei fließend, ungehindert und einzigartig. Die hier präsentierte Sammlung von Werken westlicher und koreanischer Künstler bietet von beidem ein bisschen.

Die poetische Bewegung, wie man sie in den Werken der koreanischen Künstler findet, stellt weitgehend eine meditative, spirituell bedingte Wiederholung dar; sie wurzelt in der ostasiatischen Philosophie und entspricht einer Ästhetik, die in der traditionellen Pinselmalerei des Ostens offenkundig ist. Der individuelle Ansatz der einzelnen Künstler zeigt sich in der Unterschiedlichkeit ihres Schaffens, doch gleichzeitig gibt es in ihrer koreanischen Identität eine kontemplative Reinheit und ein poetisches Empfinden, die sie miteinander verbinden. Dieses moderne lyrische Gefühl, das oft mit Nostalgie durchtränkt ist, pulsiert rhythmisch durch die östlichen wie westlichen Techniken und Materialien, die sie auf vielfältige Weise verwenden. Viele dieser aus Korea stammenden Künstler haben ja lange Phasen ihres Lebens studierend und arbeitend in westlichen Ländern verbracht, doch alle haben nach wie vor enge Verbindungen zu ihrer Heimat. Deshalb vermochte der erhebliche Einfluss westlicher Kunstauffassungen und Stile, dem sie ausgesetzt waren, ihre koreanische Identität auch nicht aufzuweichen, vielmehr hat er sie gestärkt.

Die künstlerischen Leistungen aller in dieser Ausstellung vertretenen Künstler – aus welchem Land sie auch stammen mögen – verbinden uns mit ihren individuellen Lebenswegen, reproduzieren auf exquisite Weise die Rhythmen und die Harmonie ihrer zeitlichen und räumlichen Präsenz und bringen die kulturellen Traditionen, aus denen sie kommen, zum Schwingen – gewissermaßen als Aufforderung, uns mit ihnen im Gleichklang zu bewegen.

Georg Baselitz

Alexander Calder

Sam Francis

Rebecca Horn

Robert Indiana

Roy Lichtenstein

Sigmar Polke

Robert Rauschenberg

Gerhard Richter

Frank Stella

I Shall Go Back

I shall go back again to the bleak shore
And build a little shanty on the sand
In such a way that the extremest band
Of brittle seaweed shall escape my door
But by a yard or two; and nevermore
Shall I return to take you by the hand.
I shall be gone to what I understand,
And happier than I ever was before.
The love that stood a moment in your eyes,
The words that lay a moment on your tongue,
Are one with all that in a moment dies,
A little under-said and over-sung.
But I shall find the sullen rocks and skies
Unchanged from what they were when I was young.

- Edna St. Vincent Millay

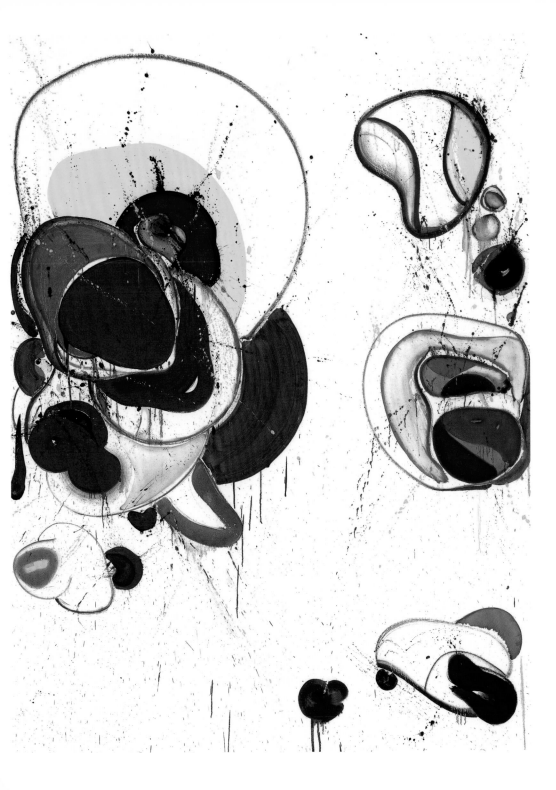

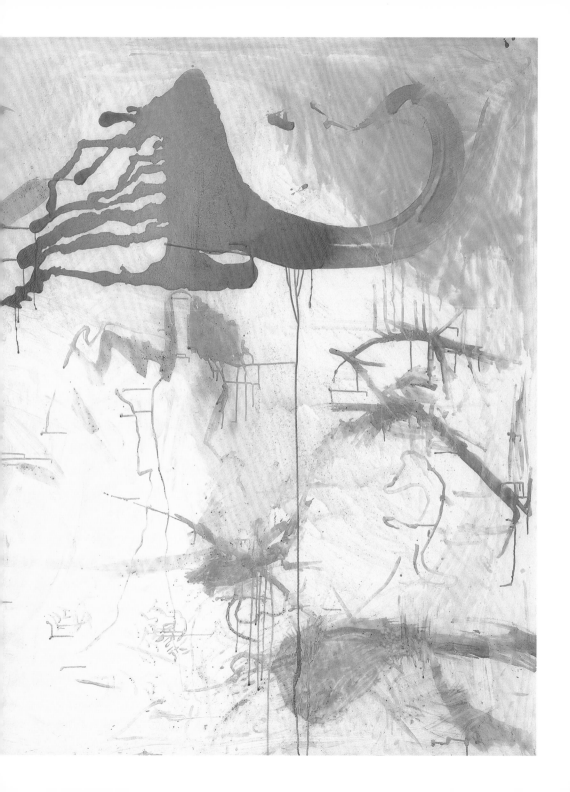

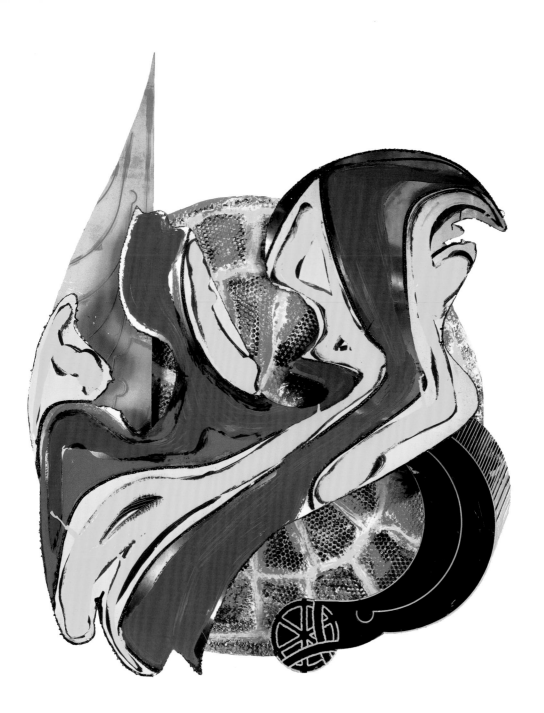

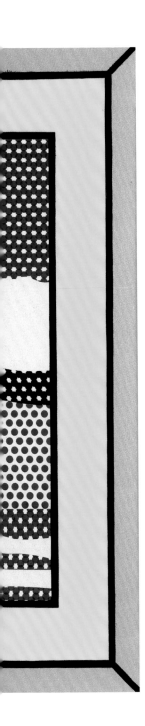

RAUSCHENBERG   '98

The World is too Much with Us

The world is too much with us; late and soon,

Getting and spending, we lay waste our powers;

Little we see in nature that is ours;

We have given our hearts away, a sordid boon!

This Sea that bares her bosom to the moon,

The winds that will be howling at all hours,

And are up-gathered now like sleeping flowers,

For this, for everything, we are out of tune;

It moves us not, -Great God! I'd rather be

A Pagon suckled in a creed outworn

So might I, standing on this pleasant lea,

Have glimpses that would make me less forlorn;

Have sight of Proteus rising from the sea;

Or hear Old Tritan blow his wreathed horn.

-William Wordsworth

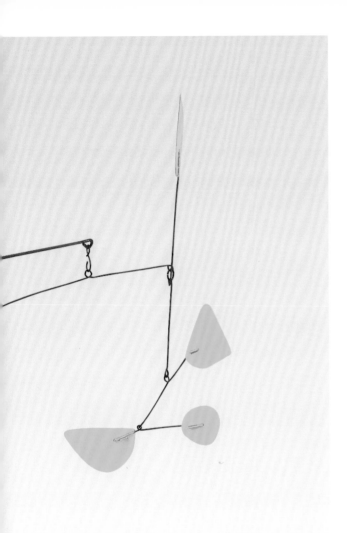

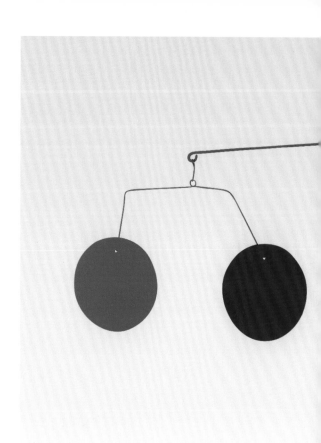

Hope is the Thing with Feathers

Hope is the thing with feathers
That perches in the soul,
And sings the tune without the words,
And never stops at all,

And sweetest in the gale is heard;
And sore must be the storm
That could abash the little bird
That kept so many warm.

I've heard it in the chillest land,
And on the strangest sea;
Yet, never, in extremity,
It asked a crumb of me.

- Emily Dickinson

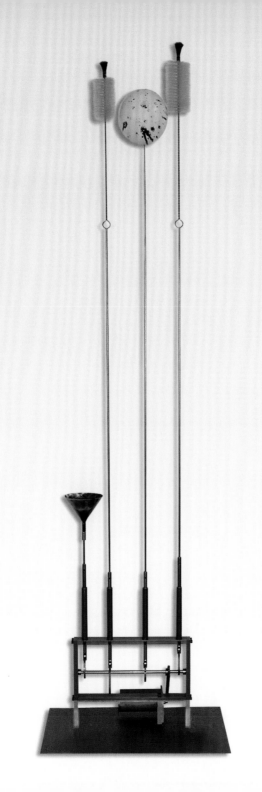

Sang-Hwa Chung

Tschang-Yeul Kim

Whan-Ki Kim

Ufan Lee

Sang-Kyoon Noh

John Pai

Nam-June Paik

Seo-Bo Park

Sung-Hy Shin

Se-Ok Suh

Time is..

Time is..

Too Slow for those who Wait

Too Swift for those who Fear

Too Long for those who Grieve

Too Short for those who Rejoice

But for those who Love

Time is not.

- Henry Van Dyke

I Live Not in Myself

I live not in myself, but I become
Portion of that around me; and to me
High mountains are a feeling, but the hum
Of human cities torture: I can see
Nothing to loathe in nature, save to be
A link reluctant in a fleshly chain,
Classed among creatures, when the soul can flee,
And with the sky, the peak, the heaving plain
Of ocean, or the stars, mingle, and not in vain.

- George Gordon, Lord Byron

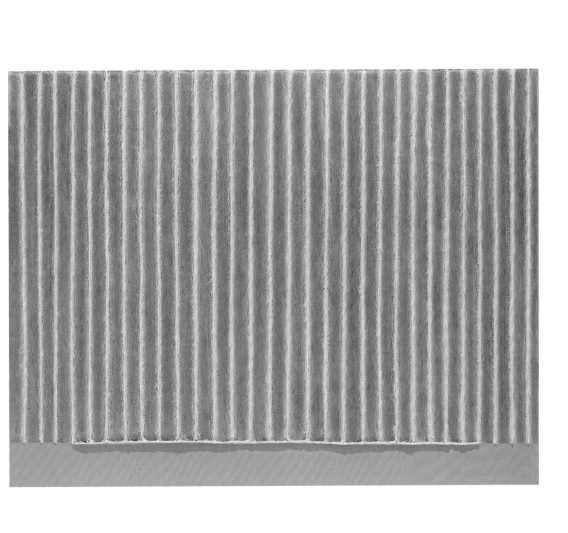

The Moon

When I see [Reality's] shadow
Thrown into the emptiness of space,
How boldly defined
The moon
Of the autumnal night!

- An anonymous author

Circle

Eat this and have a cup of tea.

- An anonymous author

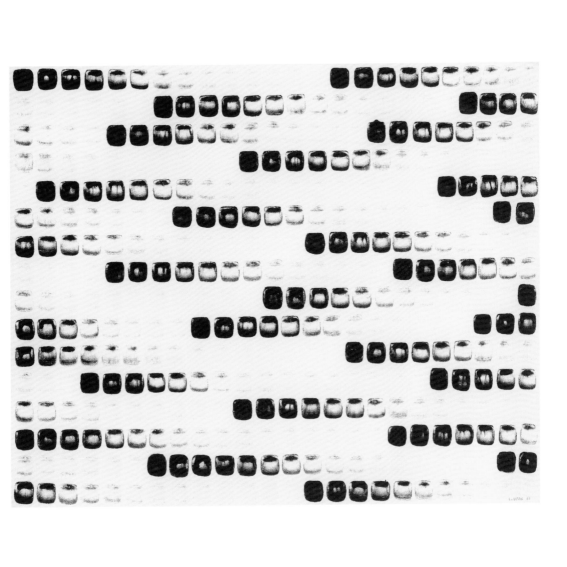

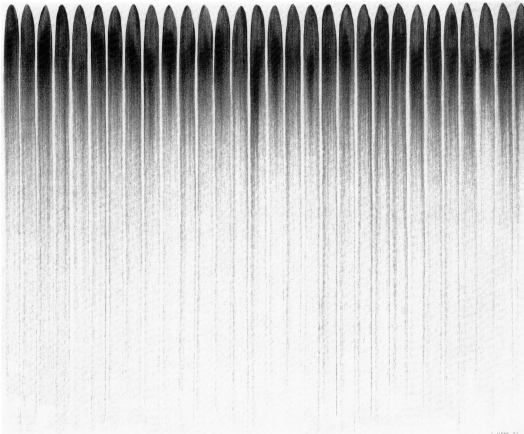

The Coming of Wisdom with Time

Through leaves are many, the root is one;
Through all the lying days of my youth
I swayed my leaves and flowers in the sun;
Now I may wither into the truth

- *William Butler Yeats*

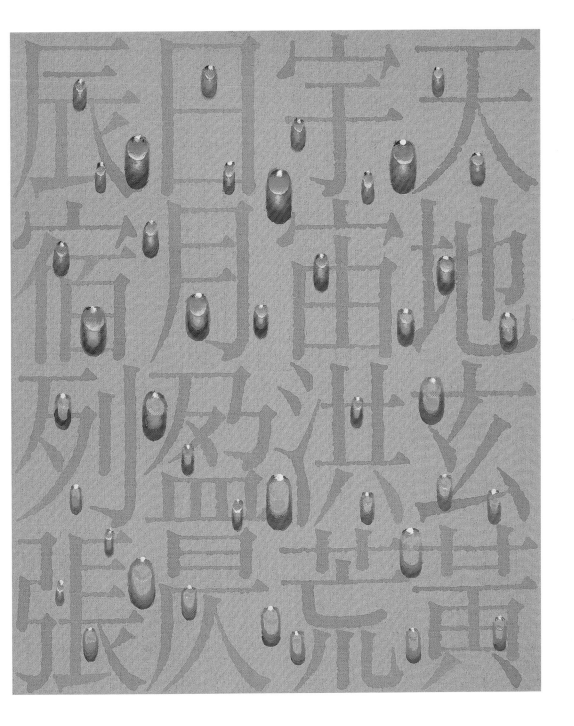

I Miss You
even though You are Beside Me

There is not water only

In the water

There is not only sky

In the sky

Not only me

In me

One who is in me

Who stirs me inside

Who flows inside me like water and sky

Meets my secret dream

I miss you even though you are beside me

- Shiva Ryu

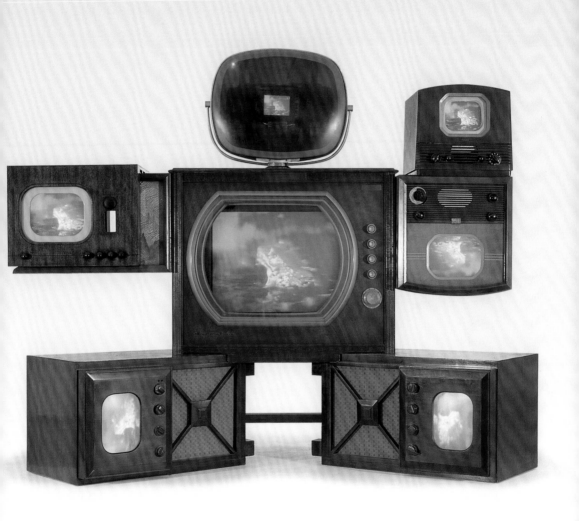

Artists
&
Art Works

Georg Baselitz (b. 1938)

A leading figure in the Neo-Expressionist movement, Georg Baselitz studied painting in East Germany and moved to West Germany in 1957. Since his first one-man exhibition in 1963 at Galerie Werner in Berlin, Baselitz has become one of Germany's best-known artists. His images are painted with a slashing intensity reminiscent of both German Expressionism and Abstract Expressionism. Crudely drawn, aggressive, and frequently disturbing, his works incorporate semi-abstract human figures, animals, and landscape elements. These images are often painted upside down to empty them of literal meaning and usually project a sense of hostility or isolation. The "upside-down-ness" of Baselitz's work is the most obvious and provocative feature of his paintings, it is, in the end, an artistic challenge that the artist sets for himself. By doing so, he explores the interface between representational and abstract art. He deliberately inverts his images in order to compel himself, and the viewer, to focus on the purely abstract aspects of the composition. Upended, the subject loses much of its usual meaning. As a result the artist is able to exploit the tension between abstraction and representation. The viewer may choose to concentrate on the expressive brushwork, vibrant colors and bold forms of the painting but will always remain aware of the unsettling presence of the human figure.

Fingermalerei-Moewe, 1972
Oil on Canvas, 170×140cm (p.43)

Der Abgarkopf, 1984
Oil on Canvas, 125×100cm (p.45)

Solo Exhibitions (Selected)

2007   *Georg Baselitz*, Museo d'Arte Moderna, Lugano, Italy

2006   *Georg Baselitz*, Fred Jahn Studio - Kunsthandel, Munich, Germany

2005   *Von Spitzweg bis Baselitz - Streifzüge durch die Sammlung Würth*, Museum Würth, Künzelsau, Germany

2004   *Aquarelles monumentales*, Fonds Régional d'Art Contemporain Picardie,

Amiens, France

2000   *Outside*, Gagosian Gallery, London, UK
        Georg Baselitz - Le Beau Style, Cabinet des Estampes, Musée d'Art et Histoire, Geneva, Switzerland

Group Exhibitions (Selected)

2007   *Poetry in Motion*, Galerie Beyeler, Basel, Switzerland ; Gallery HYUNDAI, Seoul, Korea

2006   *Eye on Europe - Prints, Books & Multiples, 1960 to Now*, Museum of Modern Art, New York, USA

2005   *Highlights*, Statens Museum for Kunst, Copenhagen, Denmark

2004   *Vision einer Sammlung*,

Museum der Moderne Salzburg, Salzburg, Austria

2003   *Expressiv*, Fondation Beyeler, Riehen/Basel, Switzerland

2001   *Collaborations with Parkett: 1984 to Now*, Museum of Modern Art, New York, USA

Alexander Calder (1898-1976)

Ranking among the most inventive artists of the twentieth century, Alexander Calder worked in many different mediums, from wire to oil paints, and produced an astonishingly varied body of work. His aesthetic sensibility was formed in Paris in the late 1920s under the influence of the European avant-garde. In Paris, he began creating small three-dimensional sculptures of circus figures made from wire, wood and cloth; over the next few years, his works became more and more abstract. Eventually, he designed sculptures with painted elements that moved mechanically, and then went on to produce pieces that moved with the air. He called these free-moving, hanging sculptures "mobiles." Though his mobiles are carefully constructed and balanced with precision, their compositions are determined by random wind currents. He used common industrial materials to create elegant and often delicate mobiles. What unites these disparate creations is Calder's wit and fundamental reliance on motion-either actual or implied-which imbue all his work with the vitality of a living organism.

Untitled, 1972, Painted Metal
71×104×25cm (p.38-39)

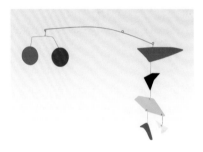

Enseign de Lunettes, 1976, Painted Sheet Metal and Wire, 96.5×137.2×25.4cm (p.40-41)

Solo Exhibitions (Selected)

2006 *Surreal Calder*, San Francisco Museum of Modern Art, San Francisco, USA

2005 *Family Loan*, Museum of Contemporary Art Chicago, Chicago, USA

2003 Museo Guggenheim Bilbao, Bilbao, Spain

2002 *Alexander Calder Motion and Color*, Nagoya City Art Museum, Nagoya, Japan

2000 *Alexander Calder in Focus*, Museum of Contemporary Art, Chicago, USA

1998 *Alexander Calder: 1898-1976*, National Gallery of Art, Washington DC, USA

1996 *Retrospective*, Musée d'Art Moderne de la Ville de Paris, Paris, France

Group Exhibitions (Selected)

2007 *Poetry in Motion*, Galerie Beyeler, Basel, Switzerland ; Gallery HYUNDAI, Seoul, Korea

2006 *Degas to Picasso - Modern Masters*, Museum of Fine Arts Boston, Boston, USA

2004 *Calder & Miro, series et projets communs 1920-1947*, Fondation Beyeler – Riehen/Basel, Switzerland

2003 *Vital Forms: American Art and Design in the Atomic Age, 1940-1960*, Phoenix Art Museum, Phoenix, USA

1997 *Made in France 1947-1997, 50 ans de création en France*, Musée National d'Art Moderne, Centre National d'Art et de Culture Georges Pompidou, Paris, France

Sam Francis (1923-1994)

Sam Francis holds a prominent position in post-war American painting. Although associated with the Abstract Expressionist movement and Clement Greenberg's Post-Painterly Abstraction, unlike many American painters of the time he had direct and prolonged exposure to French painting and to Japanese art which had an individual impact on his work. He studied botany, medicine and psychology at the University of California, Berkeley and served in the United States Air Force during World War II before being injured in a plane crash. He was in the hospital for several years, and it was while there that he began to paint. Once out of the hospital he returned to Berkeley, this time to study art. Francis was initially influenced by the work of abstract expressionists such as Mark Rothko, Arshile Gorky and Clyfford Still. He spent the 1950s in Paris, having his first exhibition there in 1952. While there he became associated with Tachisme. He later spent time in Japan, and some have seen an influence from Zen Buddhism in his work. Francis spent some time in Paris executing entirely monochromatic works, but his mature pieces are generally large oil paintings with splashed or splattered areas of bright contrasting color.

Untitled, 1991, Acrylic on Paper
119×119cm (p.23)

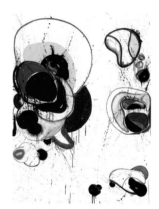

Why Then Opened II, 1962-63
Oil on Canvas, 243×183cm (p.25)

Rebecca Horn (b.1944)

Rebecca Horn is one of the most illustrious contemporary German artists working with drawing, sculpture, installation, kinetics, photography, performance, action, video, film and text. She has been working with various media simultaneously for some time and not since the 'crossover' has become a fad in the art scene of today. She designs and makes instruments used to present the human body. In her works, Horn conducts a multi-layer discourse on nature, culture, and technology issues. Often she employs mythological illusions. The fundamental topic of her work is human hypersensitivity, emotions, obsessions and fears.

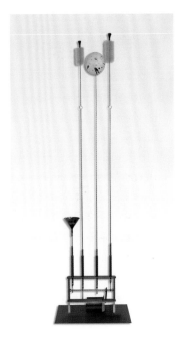

Staussen Universum - Zärtlich, 2007
Brass, Steel, Motor, Electronic, Egg of an
Ostrich, 192×66×40cm (p.47)

Robert Indiana (b.1928)

Robert Indiana, one of the foremost American Pop artists, has produced a significant body of work since the 1960's, focusing on the potential of simple linguistic elements and techniques. Indiana's early experiments with severely planned forms led in 1960 to his distinctive brand of pop painting, which combines stenciled lettering with clearly defined areas of bright color. He uses standardized fonts and stenciled text arranging numbers, letters and simple words and phrases in graphic configurations. The bold colors and forms employ a directness and legibility that typically characterize advertisements and design. Indiana's sculptures make language physical, giving its form as a signifier and the ideas and concepts it signifies material presence. Displayed in either groups or as individual works, the sculptures address the temporal dimension of experience. The numbers can be moved and organized in a random configuration or as a series making the sequence of our observations. Numbers organize and quantify information, and Indiana's sculptures give these abstract concepts a specific concrete form. Since the late 1960s he has expanded his LOVE theme to a series of sculptures, some of them monumental in size. Indiana is a democratic artist: he appeals to our basic means of communication and experience, and this undoubtedly contributes to his accessibility and success.

Art, 2000, Painted Aluminium
45.8×45.8×22.9cm (p.19)

LOVE, 1966-1998, Stainless Steel
121.9×121.9×61 (p.21)

Roy Lichtenstein (1923-1997)

Roy Lichtenstein was a prominent American Pop artist, whose work borrowed heavily from popular advertising and comic book styles, which he himself described as being "as artificial as possible." His paintings reflect modern typographic and printing techniques such as Ben-Day dots and make innovative use of commonplace imagery. Taking a specific style as his starting point, from the Neoplasticism of Mondrian to the fragmented planes of Cubism, Lichtenstein approaches Modern art as a compendium of ready-made procedures. Yet unlike his comic-strip paintings, Lichtenstein's riffs on art history are based on instantly recognizable shorthand for each period rather than any specific painting. His work of the 1970s largely consisted of ironic reinterpretations of well-known paintings by famous painters. His paintings of the 1980s and 90s, which often include both real and simulated brush strokes, are typified by the large canvas figures in a landscape.

Reflections : Untitled, 1988, Oil and Magna on Canvas
107 × 127.5cm (p.32-33)

Sigmar Polke (b.1941)

Sigmar Polke is one of the most significant painters of the post-war generation, yet his career has by no means been confined to painting. Since the early 1960s he has experimented with a wide range of styles and subject matter, bringing together imagery from contradictory or unexpected sources, both historical and contemporary, and using a variety of different materials and techniques. In fact Polke's artistic diversity, and his resistance to any form of categorization, has been seen as the only consistent theme in his work. Polke's paintings from the late 1960s take up art as their theme, often in a humorous way. He responded with a certain sense of irony to American Pop art. His huge raster grids were inspired by Roy Lichenstein's bold Benday dots and Andy Warhol's early use of photographic transfer made its way into his work. Polke revolutionized paintings in the second half of his career by using non-art or anti-art materials and chemical substances to cover canvases. These mutable and magical works had Polke earn the title of "alchemical artist." His later abstract works are made of alchemical mixtures of silver nitrate, resins, meteor particles, and unstable pigments, among other non-art materials. The medium of such works suggests both the poisons of industrial by-products and the magic of alchemical change.

Silberbild, 1990, Silvernitrate, Silverbromide, Silversulphate on Linen, 200×190cm (p.26-27)

Silberbild, 1990, Silvernitrate, Silverbromide, Silversulphate on Canvas, 200×190cm (p.28-29)

Robert Rauschenberg (b. 1925)

One of the most influential American artists of this century, Robert Rauschenberg possesses an indefatigable zeal for fusing real life with art. He is often seen as enabling a transition from Abstract Expressionism to the media-saturated surfaces of Pop. For the last fifty years, his art has encompassed all manner of experimentation and a vast array of media, including silk screening, printmaking and photography. He is perhaps most famous for his 'Combines' of the 1950s, in which all kinds of non-traditional materials and objects were employed in rich and innovative combinations. In 1962 Rauschenberg made his first lithographs and silkscreens and has been involved with innovative print making since then. His combinations of disparate images made through photo-transfer, silkscreen, incorporation of found objects, and painted forms resulted in striking juxtapositions. He has experimented with discs, motors, Plexiglas, sound, and variations in techniques in the transfer of photographs to silk-screened editioned works of art. The interplay of activity in different media is at the core of his work, which has been marked throughout his career by a sense of experiment and exploration.

Untitled, 1988, Mixed Media Collage
107×80cm (p.35)

Page 50, Paragraph 6 (Short Stories), 2000
Vegetable Dye Transfer, Pigment Transfer,
Acrylic and Graphite on Polylaminate
217.2×153.7cm (p.37)

Solo Exhibitions (Selected)

2007 Robert Rauschenberg,
Moderna Museet,
Stockholm, Sweden
2006 Vonderbank art galleries,
Berlin, Germany
2005 Robert Rauschenberg-
Combines, The Metropolitan
Museum of Art, New York,
USA
2003 Short Stories,
Pace Wildenstein, New York,
USA

2002 Fondation Dina Vierny,
Musée Maillol, Paris, France
2000 Robert Rauschenberg -
Synapsis Shuffle, Whitney
Museum of American Art,
New York, USA
1997 Solomon R. Guggenheim
Museum, New York, USA

Group Exhibitions (Selected)

2007 Poetry in Motion, Galerie
Beyeler, Basel, Switzerland ;
Gallery HYUNDAI, Seoul,
Korea
2006 Speaking with Hands,
Moscow Museum of Modern
Art, Moscow, Russia
2005 EXIT- Ausstieg aus dem Bild,
Museum für Neue Kunst &
Medienmuseum, Karlsruhe,
Germany
2004 Pop from San Francisco

Collections, San Francisco
Museum of Modern Art, San
Francisco, USA
2002 Popcorn and Politics -
Activists of Art, Kiasma
Museum of Contemporary
Art, Helsinki, Finland

Gerhard Richter (b. 1932)

A German artist who refuses to settle down in one artistic style, Gerhard Richter, his artistic style can be categorized into three stages: Photo-Paintings (concentrating on realistically expressing amateur photos and photos in newspapers), Color Charts (recording the traces and marks of organic actions and project and magnified them by using photographic techniques), and Abstract Paintings (featuring complex composition and colors). The artist who was affected by Socialist Realist of East Germany began to experience various modern art genres including American Abstract art after moving to Düsseldorf and this was the decisive factor

Tisch, 1982, Oil on Canvas, 225×294cm (p.48-49)

that produced his artistic style in early days that passed over the boundaries between abstract and figurative arts. After all, his works discover the possibility of fusing photos and paintings and reach the stage of double denial by reproducing existing photographic images while rejecting practices of pictorial art and at the same time, denying photographic art through adopting actions of pictorial art. Each stage of his artistic work is not only another piece of work but also is a great adventure meaning to transcend Modernism by overturning the concept of artistic uniqueness and dichromatic division of paintings and non-paintings all presented by Modernism as a part of the process of breaking down the boundary between photographs and paintings.

Solo Exhibitions (Selected)

2006   Gerhard Richter, Neues Museum Weserburg Bremen, Bremen, Germany

2005   K21 Kunstsammlung im Ständehaus, Düsseldorf, Germany

2003   Gerhard Richter: Forty Years of Painting, Hirshhorn Museum and Sculpture Garden, Washington DC, USA

2002   Gerhard Richter: 40 years of painting, Museum of Modern Art, New York , USA

2001   Gerhard Richter: Malerei 1966-1998, Zeppelin Museum Friedrichshafen, Friedrichshafen, Germany

Group Exhibitions (Selected)

2007   Poetry in Motion, Galerie Beyeler, Basel, Switzerland ; Gallery HYUNDAI, Seoul, Korea

2004   Contre-images, Carré d'Art, Musée d'art Contemporain, Nîmes, France

2002   Claude Monet...bis zum digitalen Impressionismus, Fondation Beyeler, Riehen/ Basel, Switzerland

2001   Collaborations with Parkett:

1984 to Now, Museum of Modern Art, New York, USA

2000   Die Intelligenz der Hand - Europäische Meisterzeichnungen von Picasso bis Beuys, Rupertinum, Museum für Moderne Kunst, Salzburg, Austria

Frank Stella (b.1936)

Frank Stella originally painted in an Abstract Expressionist style but then later expressed the precision and rationality that characterized minimalism, employing parallel angular stripes to emphasize the rectangular shape of his large canvases in his early "black paintings". His innovative and influential use of irregularly shaped canvases first appeared in his metallic series in 1960. Later examples of his work had more emphasis on color in decorative curved motifs. In the 1970s and 80s, Stella abandoned the minimalist aesthetic in favor of a more improvised, dynamic, and dramatic idiom in mixed-media. It was during this period that Stella departed from "flat" paintings and instead created large, jutting, multipart, three-dimensional painting-constructions that often incorporate bright colors, enlarged versions of French curves, and lively brushstroke patterns. Stella's work became fully three-dimensional in the early 1990s in a series of dense abstract sculptures composed of found and cast elements in stainless steel and bronze. These unpainted and often large-scale metal wall constructions, with their tangled, layered, and looping shapes, project an air of vibrant spontaneity

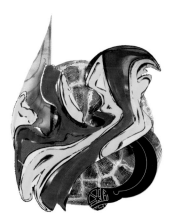

The Try-Works, 1988, Relief Mixed Media
124.5×110.5×58cm (p.31)

Solo Exhibitions [Selected]

2006 *Frank Stella – 1958*, The Menil Collection, Houston, USA

2005 *Frank Stella - Moby Dick Series*, Museo Nacional de Bellas Artes, Santiago, Chile

2004 *Frank Stella - A Breakthrough In Abstraction - Exotic Birds*, Gagosian Gallery - New York, USA

2003 *Frank Stella*, The Nagoya City Art Museum, Nagoya, Japan

1999 *Frank Stella at 2000 - Changing The Rules*, Museum of Contemporary Art – North Miami, Miami, USA

1987 *Frank Stella: Works from 1970 to 1987*, MoMA Museum of Modern Art, New York, USA

Group Exhibitions [Selected]

2007 *Poetry in Motion*, Galerie Beyeler, Basel, Switzerland ; Gallery HYUNDAI, Seoul, Korea

2006 *The Persistence of Geometry*, Museum of Contemporary Art Cleveland, Cleveland, USA

2005 *Singular Forms (Sometimes Repeated) - Art from 1951 to the Present*, Solomon R. Guggenheim Museum, New York, USA

2002 *Lichtenstein, Motherwell, Stella*, National Gallery of Australia, Canberra, Australia

1998 *Artists and Subjects: Picasso to Stella*, Museum of Modern Art, New York, USA

Sang-Hwa Chung (b.1932)

Since the 1970s, Sang-Hwa Chung has consistently developed a unique concept and technique, in which a method of 'Peeling' and 'Layering' is employed as a form of painting on canvas. Five centimeters of thick zinc paint is first layered onto the canvas. When it has completely dried, the canvas is then folded horizontally and vertically so that the surface of the canvas has checkered cracks on it. Afterwards, the zinc paint is peeled off from the numerous square-shaped cracks one by one, and then several layers of acrylic paint are coated onto it. Through this complicated process, Chung has been able to achieve special 'mosaic' patterns in his works. Ultimately, he has created modern pieces of work with his inter-connective acrylic squares through a systematic and repetitive process. These productions of minimal art are created with a unique Korean style along with a touch of structuralism. Another noteworthy aspect about Chung's art is that all the repeated folding, peeling, and layering is done alone without any assistance, requiring a great deal of time and effort. Most of his pieces are left 'Untitled' because Chung believes the repeated process of his art is in and of itself the work of art. In other words, his art speaks for itself through the repeated process of its creation rather than as a sole finished product.

Untitled 05-7-15, 2005, Acrylic on Canvas
162.2×130.3cm (p.77)

Untitled 05-2-14, 2005, Acrylic on Canvas
162.2×130.3cm (p.78)

Tschang-Yeul Kim (b.1929)

Tschang-Yeul Kim is renowned for his "waterdrops". The discovery of the water drops was a blessed accident for Kim. He was inspired with the idea while spraying water onto his works and seeing the water drops glittering in the sunlight. However, it was during the winter of 1972-1973 that his actual water drop art was born. Kim, then, devoted himself to the creation of a new organic form and similar representations by reducing the use of bright colors. The water drops are luminous and sharply defined, and appear deceptively wet and real; the beauty of these water drops is that they deceive the eye. Letters began to appear in Kim's work in 1975 and by 1983 small sized Chinese characters from the "Classic-Thousand-Characters" filled up his canvases. From 1987, Kim launched the full-scale use of Chinese characters as backgrounds for his water drops. The transition of water drops into installation art, which included three-dimensional crystal ellipsoids placed on top of a hexahedral trapezoid of cemented sand, was first shown in his solo exhibition held at Enrico Navarra Gallery in Paris in 1993.

Waterdrops, 2000, Oil on Sand
162.2×130.3cm (p.81)

Recurrence, 1997, Oil on Canvas
73×60cm (p.83)

Whan-Ki Kim (1913-1974)

In the early part of his career, Whan-Ki Kim experimented with two-dimensional composition, adopting objects, such as large vases, mountains, and old-fashioned Korean stone walls. Using simple forms and transparent colors, he recreated typical Korean images. From the mid-1960s, when Whanki began to reside in New York, his paintings became noticeably more abstract as the shapes turned more geometrical. From 1970 to 1974, the year of his death, Whanki devoted himself to a dots series, which is widely viewed today as his most important achievement. He began to render countless dots flickering in between checkered lines, each dot documenting his own stories of nostalgia. Though on the surface they may seem to be just dots lined up, their creator saw them as stories from his heart. In the last year of his life, the blue dot series turned darker, into blackish blue and gray, and this created white lines dividing the canvas. The transition to black is more than just that, however. The black represents the black chaos, which is talked about in oriental philosophy. In this respect, Kim's dot series in the 1970s is considered the heart of Kim's works personally and served as a turning point in Korean contemporary painting.

Untitled 12-V-70, 1970, Oil on Cotton
235 × 167cm (p.53)

Untitled, 1970's, Oil on Cotton, 62 × 50cm (p.55)

Solo Exhibitions (Selected)

2004 *The 30th Anniversary Exhibition of the Death of Whanki*, Whanki Museum, Seoul, Korea

1987 *Whanki: Ten Years in New York*, Centre national des arts plastiques, Paris, France

1975 *Retrospective*, National Museum of Contemporary Art, Seoul, Korea

1971-73 Poindexter Gallery, New York, USA

1957 M.Benezit Gallery, Paris, France
      Cheval de Verre Gallery, Brussels, Belgium

1956 M.Benezit Gallery, Paris, France

1937 Amigo Gallery, Tokyo, Japan

Group Exhibitions (Selected)

2007 *Poetry in Motion*, Galerie Beyeler, Basel, Switzerland ; Gallery HYUNDAI, Seoul, Korea

2006 Gallery HYUNDAI, Seoul, Korea

1972 National Museum of Contemporary Art, Seoul, Korea

1965 *One Man Exhibition in Special Room*, 8th São Paulo Biennale, Brazil

196   7th São Paulo Biennale, Brazil

1957 *Artists in Paris*, Monaco

1956 *Artists in Paris*, Italy

1937-40 Liberty Artists Association, Tokyo, Japan

1936 Baik Man Hwoe(White Barbarians), Tokyo, Japan

Ufan Lee (b.1936)

Philosophical ideas are central to Ufan Lee's artistic practice. He was a leading member of the "Mono-Ha" group during the late 60s. This group was the first Japanese avant-garde art movement to attract international attention. A commonly shared characteristic of the artists associated with the Mono-Ha group was their rejection of traditional notions of representation and, in particular, the rejection of the principle that art expresses the artist's personal experience. They sought instead to minimize expression and to focus on the observed reality of the artwork as well as the internal relations of its parts. This concept is a mainstay of Lee's approach. In his ⟨From Point⟩ and ⟨From Line⟩ series in the 1980's, Lee used the repetition of discrete marks superimposed on a blank ground to convey a sense of infinity. His paintings belong to an extended series of related works that explore the same theme. In the late 1980's, his interests shifted in the ⟨From Winds⟩ and ⟨With Winds⟩ series. Currently he is working on a series titled ⟨Correspondence⟩.The blend of Western and Eastern traditions in all of Lee's series contain the delicacy of the East Asian calligraphic style.

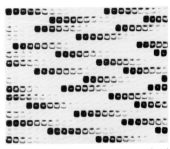

From Point, 1980, Oil on Canvas, 80×100cm (p.73)

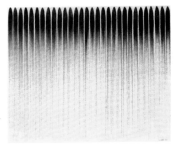

From Line, 1982, Oil on Canvas, 80×100cm (p.75)

Solo Exhibitions [Selected]

2005 Musée d'Art Moderne, Saint-Etienne, France
2001 Kunstmuseum Bonn, Bonn, Germany
2000 Galerie m, Bochum, Germany
1998 Nigata City Museum, Nigata, Japan
1997 Galerie Nationale du Jeu de Paume, Paris, France
1996 Lisson Gallery, London, UK
1993 The Museum of Modern Art Kamakura, Kamakura, Japan
1988 Padiglione D'Arte Contemporanea, Milano, Italy

Group Exhibitions [Selected]

2007 *Poetry in Motion*, Galerie Beyeler, Basel, Switzerland ; Gallery HYUNDAI, Seoul, Korea
2006 *La force de l'art*, Grand Palais, Paris, France
2003 *Happiness*, Mori Art Museum, Tokyo, Japan
2001 *Century City*, Tate Modern, London, UK
1994 *Scream against the sky*, Guggenheim Soho Museum, New York, USA
1992 *Contemporary Art from Korea*, Tate Gallery, Liverpool, UK
1987 *Painting 1977-87*, The National Museum of Art, Osaka, Japan
1986 *Mono-ha*, Kamakura Gallery, Tokyo, Japan

Sang-Kyoon Noh (b.1958)

Sang-Kyoon Noh has been using sequins as his main medium for more than a decade. Noh's childhood experience motivated him to use sequins, which are not often used in art works. He began to see life in a new light when he was rescued at the point of almost drowning. While pawing at the air to get out of the water, he thought that he would die being nobody or nothing and without any purpose, just like a fish. In his early works, the surface of sequins arranged on the canvas through repetition of conscious and unconscious acts finds its way out of symbolizing fish and reaches out to the vast expanse of the cosmos. The objects of Noh's sequined works have expanded from plane canvases to ready-made three-dimensional objects. By covering the lower body part of plastic mannequins and Buddhist statues, or handkerchiefs and tents hung in the air with sequins in a meticulous manner, the artist hides the natural characters and textures of the objects and instead gives them a whole new meaning. The method he has adopted, constantly 'attaching' ready-made sequins to canvases or objects, requires tremendous physical efforts, time and energy. For him, this act of 'attaching' sequins, which are absolutely materials and objects, to the limited space within the frame of canvases kept the artist from letting go off the question 'Did pictorial art die in my art world?'.

For the Worshipers, 2006, Sequins on the Buddha Statue of Polyester Resin and Fiberglass, 110×88.5×64cm (p.85)

Another End, 1997, Sequins on Canvas 218×218cm (p.86)

Solo Exhibitions [Selected]

2004   Bryce Wolkowitz Gallery, New York, USA
2002   Gallery E.S., Tokyo, Japan
2000   Robert Sandelson gallery, London, UK
       National Museum of Contemporary Art, Gwachon, Korea
1999   Claudia Gian Ferrari, Milan, Italy
1998   Kumho Museum of Art, Seoul, Korea

1992   Higgins Hall Gallery, New York, USA

Group Exhibitions [Selected]

2007   *Poetry in Motion*, Galerie Beyeler, Basel, Switzerland ; Gallery HYUNDAI, Seoul, Korea
2005   *Seoul-Until Now*, Charlottenborg Exhibition Hall, Copenhagen, Denmark
2004   *Alchemy of Daily Life*, National Museum of Contemporary Art, Gwachon, Korea
2003   *The Color of Korea*, Iwate

Museum of Art, Iwate, Japan
       East of Eden : forbidden fruit in London, 14 Wharf Road, London, UK
1999   *48th Venice Biennale*, Korean Pavilion, Venice, Italy
1994   *Modus Operandi*, Leonora Vega Gallery, New York, USA

John Pai (b.1937)

Though there is a clear ethos running through the whole, John Pai's career can be divided into three stages. The first, beginning in the early-to-mid 1960s and lasting into the early 1980s, is dominated by scientific investigation and formal structuralism. Examining nature in order to acquire his own voice, Pai broke things down to basic building blocks and worked with the 'irreducible core'. In the process, he was able to achieve certain 'complete freedom'. The second stage in Pai's work roughly spans from 1985 to the early 1990s, when the artist arrived at a new recognition of his relationship with nature. The works from this period reflect his encounters with nature. And the third stage begins around 1996 and continues to the present. He has been developing a style quite distinct from the previous stages, and the works from this period seem to belong to a completely different artist. Pai explains, "I began to work with longer more continuous lines, as if I were drawing in space, bending, crimping and looping at will." Finding abstract concepts lodged in his own unconsciousness with an increasing intensity, John Pai gives form to contrasting sensibilities, such as balance and imbalance, inwardness and exteriority in his art.

Work, 1990, Steel, 98×78×60cm (p.65)

Risen, Fallen, Walkin, 1987, Welded Steel
122×107×46cm (p.67)

Solo Exhibitions (Selected)

2006 Gallery HYUNDAI, Seoul, Korea
1997 Sigma Gallery, New York, USA
1993 Gallery HYUNDAI, Seoul, Korea
1990 Souyun Yi Gallery, New York, USA
1987 Gallery Korea, New York, USA
1982 Whanki Foundation, New York, USA

1964 Pratt Institute, New York, USA
1952 Oglebay Institute, Wheeling, West Virginia, USA

Group Exhibitions (Selected)

2007 *Poetry in Motion*, Galerie Beyeler, Basel, Switzerland ; Gallery HYUNDAI, Seoul, Korea
2003 *Dream & Reality*, Contemporary Korean-American Art, Smithsonian International Gallery, Washington D.C, USA
2000 *Welded Sculpture of the 20th Century*, Neuberger Museum, Puechase, USA

1988 Bergen County Museum, New Jersey, USA
1981 *Korean Drawing Now*, Brooklyn Museum, New York, USA National Museum of Contemporary Art, Gwachon, Korea
1980 *The Great Atlanta/New York Sculpture Exchange*, Atlanta, USA

Nam-June Paik (1932-2006)

A performance and conceptual artist, Nam-June Paik, who died last year, worked mainly with video, integrating visual images with music. Paik's first artistic interest was music, which he studied at the University of Tokyo. He graduated in 1956 with a degree in aesthetics, producing a thesis on Arnold Schoenberg. Paik's studies continued in Germany at the Universities of Munich and Cologne, and the Conservatory of Music in Freiburg. During this time, he met composer John Cage, whose innovative, almost randomized sound motivated Paik's interest in garbled television noise. Cage's ideas and art had a tremendous influence on his work. With this background, he began pioneering video art as a medium. Supplementary video and ready-made television sets have become a trademark of Paik's work. From his Fluxus-based performances and altered television sets of the early 1960s, to his ground-breaking videotapes and multi-media installations of the 1970s, 80s and 90s, Paik made an enormous contribution to the history and development of video as an art form. As a major contemporary artist and a seminal figure in video art, his video sculptures, installations, performances and tapes encompass one of the most influential and significant bodies of work in the medium.

TV is New Heart, 1989, Mixed Media
200×180×50cm (p.89)

Fat Boy Buddha, 1999, Mixed Media
213×91×152cm (p.91)

Solo Exhibitions [Selected]

2006   *Homage to Nam June Paik*, Leeum Samsung Museum, Seoul, Korea

2005   *Nam June Paik*, Orange County Museum of Art, Newport Beach, USA

2004   *Nam June Paik-Global Groove 2004*, Deutsche Guggenheim, Berlin, Germany

2000   *The World of Nam June Paik*, Guggenheim Museum, New York, USA

1999   *Nam June Paik : Fluxus/Video*, Kunsthalle Bremen, Bremen, Germany

1995   *Nam June Paik : Art&Communication*, Gallery HYUNDAI ; Galerie BHAK, Seoul, Korea

1994   Fukuoka Art Museum, Fukuoka, Japan

1993   *Feedback & Feedforth*, Watari Museum, Tokyo, Japan

Group Exhibitions [Selected]

2007   *Poetry in Motion*, Galerie Beyeler, Basel, Switzerland ; Gallery HYUNDAI, Seoul, Korea

2006   *Collection on View*, Hirshhorn Museum and Sculpture Garden, Washington, DC, USA

1999   *The American Century : Art and Culture, 1900-2000 (Part2)*, Whitney Museum of American Art, New York, USA

1996   *Videoscape*, Guggenheim Museum, New York, USA

1995   *Asiana*, Palazzo Vendramin, Paris, France

1992   *Fluxus Attitudes*, New York Museum of Contemporary Art, New York, USA

Seo-Bo Park (b.1931)

During the momentous times of the Korean modern art movement, Seo-Bo Park was considered as a leading figure. His works between the late 1950s and the early 1960s are known to have contributed significantly to the development and acceptance of Western Informel art in Korea. Park's works from the early 1970s up to now featuring a monochrome artistic style are highly regarded as interpretation of Western Minimalism from a Korean perspective. Park's artistic style has undergone several changes over his long career and can be classified into three stages from the Informel stage represented by his 〈Protoplasm〉 series of the late 1950s to the visual abstraction and virtual image stage represented by the 〈Idioplasm〉 series of the late 1960s and finally to the famous 〈Ecriture〉 stage that began in the early 1970s. The 〈Ecriture〉 series, which make up two-thirds of Park's life work, can further be divided into two stages. The first 〈Ecriture〉 period concentrates on the repetition of dense pencil lines drawn in oblique patterns. In the latter 〈Ecriture〉 period, Park meticulously applies by hand Hanji, traditional Korean mulberry paper, to the canvas, which adds a textural quality unique to the artistic medium and to his contemporary artistic achievement.

Ecriture, 2000, Mixed Media with Korean Paper
72.7×60.6cm (p.61)

Ecriture, 2006 Mixed Media with Korean Paper
40×54cm (p.63)

Sung-Hy Shin (b.1948)

Sung-Hy Shin's artwork is concerned mainly with the surface of the plane as a three-dimensional object. His working process is complex. First, he paints and then tears into strips what he has painted, and then he ties what he has torn into knots and rearranges them on the canvas. In the first stage, he spreads out a cotton cloth on the floor and paints a picture on both the front and the back. The purpose of painting the cloth on both sides is to interpret a plane as a three-dimensional object. The next step starts with the tearing of the painted cloth into strips once the painting has dried. When the cotton cloth is torn, the images in the painting die with it. In the third stage, Shin ties these objects together on the surface. He cuts and tears the surface of the canvas transforming it into gaps and crevices. Then he ties and weaves the torn cloth strips bearing the colors of the images. The tied ones form knots, while the woven ones plaits or hems, as they are reborn as a painting of relief. As the structure is tied to the surface, this "nouage" technique forms a forest of paintings, which combine substance, spirit and performance. "Nouage" is a term used by Shin. He explains "nouage" as "a technique similar to collage but somewhat different in nature". He uses this term to theorize the method of his works. His works are closely related to "Support/Surface", a trend that was widespread in France in the 1970s.

Espace vital, 1999, Acrylic on Canvas
130×130cm (p.68)

Entrelacs, 1997, Acrylic on Canvas & Linen
117×80cm (p.71)

Solo Exhibitions [Selected]

2006 Gallery Proarta, Zürich, Switzerland
2005 Gallery HYUNDAI, Seoul, Korea
2002 Gallery INAX, Tokyo, Japan
2000 Gallery Baudoin Lebon, Paris, France
1999 Andrew Shire Gallery, Los Angeles
1998 Gallery Convergence, Nantes, France
1989 National Museum of Contemporary Art, Gwacheon, Korea

Group Exhibitions [Selected]

2007 *Poetry in Motion*, Galerie Beyeler, Basel, Switzerland ; Gallery HYUNDAI, Seoul, Korea
2006 *32 artistes contemporains detournent le Blazer Renoma*, Galerie Meyer Le Bihan, Paris, France
2003 *Age of Philosophy and Esthetics*, National Museum of Contemporary Art, Gwacheon, Korea
2002 Aichi prefectural Museum of Art, ATC Museum, Iwate Museum, Japan
2001 *Tradition and Innovation I*, Korean Cultural Center, Berlin and Kronberg, Germany
1998 *80 Artistes Autour du Mondial*, Gallery Enrico Navarra, Paris, France
1992 *Korean Contemporary Painting*, Nichido Museum, Japan

Se-Ok Seo (b.1929)

Se-Ok Seo is one of the first generation of artists that was educated after the withdrawal of the Japanese imperial colonialists in 1945. He founded a group called Mouk-lim, meaning Ink-forest, which introduced avant-garde concepts in painting that explored the use of unusual techniques and forms. Although no concept of abstract art exists in traditional Asian painting, Seo managed to convince the reserved National Gallery to accept the unacceptable: the unprecedented integration of an abstract approach to traditional painting. Seo's paintings from the late 50's onward are distinctively abstract works comprised of points and lines using traditional tools. Since the 1970s, the points and lines of his abstract paintings have been transformed into simplified human forms, which have also been translated into signs. This ⟨People⟩ series has become his central work. Seo stands out from other artists in that he attempted to reinvent traditional oriental painting. The traditional oriental painting is deeply rooted in ideographic writings, which favors the use of brushes and tends to transform the elements of nature into signs. What Seo seeks to depict is not really a picture or a sign. The essence of his innovative approach to traditional painting is in achieving a holistic outcome that is not quite a hybrid of the two but more like a synthesis of the thesis and anti-thesis. Thus, Seo's art works have a double impact derived from the images and signs simultaneously created, which constantly enhance the justification of their mutual presence as if energy circulates from one to the other.

People, 1996, Ink on Rice Paper
137×173cm (p.56-57)

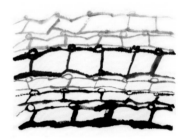

People, Ink on Rice Paper
137×173cm (p.58-59)

Solo Exhibitions (Selected)

2005 National Museum of Art Deoksugung, Seoul, Korea
1996 Gallery HYUNDAI, Seoul, Korea
FIAC, Paris, France
1989 Gallery HYUNDAI, Seoul, Korea
1985 Baruch College Gallery, New York, U.S.A
1983 Pacific Asia Museum, Pasadena, U.S.A
1979 Gallery Ueda, Tokyo, Japan
1974 Gallery HYUNDAI, Seoul, Korea
1971 Shinsegae Gallery, Seoul, Korea

Group Exhibitions (Selected)

2007 *Poetry in Motion*, Galerie Beyeler, Basel, Switzerland ; Gallery HYUNDAI, Seoul, Korea
1995 *Exhibition of Korea Modern Arts*, Paris City Art Center, Paris, France
1994 *Seoul International Contemporary Art Festival*, National Museum of Contemporary Art, Gwachon, Korea
1991 *Exhibition Tour of Korean Modern Paintings*, Yugoslavia
1986 *Exhibition of Asia Modern Indian-ink Drawings*, Assembly Hall of Fine Arts, Seoul, Korea
1985 *Modern Art 40 Years*, National Museum of Contemporary Art, Seoul, Korea
1977-78 *Europe Exhibition Tour of Contemporary Oriental Paintings by Korean Artists*, France, Sweden, Holland, Germany

Poetry in Motion

June 12th-September 15th, 2007 Galerie BEYELER
October 2nd-October 14th, 2007 Gallery HYUNDAI

GALERIE BEYELER

Bäumleingasse 9 CH-4001 Basel, Switzerland
Tel 41 61 206 97 00   Fax 41 61 206 97 19
galerie@beyeler.com   www.beyeler.com

GALLERY HYUNDAI

80 Sagan-dong, Jongno-gu, Seoul, Korea 110-190
Tel 82 2 734 6111~3   Fax 82 2 734 1616
mail@galleryhyundai.com   www.galleryhyundai.com

Catalogue and exhibition
Ernst Beyeler
Claudia Neugebauer, Karin Sutter, Francesca Volpe
Hyung-Teh Do
Sung-Eun Kim, Eun-Soo Kim
and Laurencina Farrant-Lee

Graphic design
Sumi Park, doART design, Korea

Text
Garett Marshall

German translator
Matthias Wolf, Berlin

Cover / Whan-Ki Kim, 'Untitled', 1970's